I0667873

Cracked Spaces

Pandora Lobo Estepario Productions™
Chicago/Oaxaca 2021

Cracked Spaces

M. Miranda Maloney

First Edition

ISBN—10: 1-940856-44-2
ISBN—13: 978-1-940856-44-5

Library of Congress Control Number: 2021944425
:

Acknowledgements

With gratitude to the journals and their editors who published the following poems:

"This morning," "A photograph," and "A twist" — Finalist, chapbook collection from *Under the Domestic Light*, Dancing Girl Press
"Message," "Blessed," and "Looking at Her Father" — *The Más Tequila Review*
"State of Affairs" — *BorderSenses*
"American Me" — *Xispas: Chicano Journal of Literature and Art*
"Canto: The City I Love" — excerpt from *The City I Love* chapbook published by Ranchos Press
"Beautiful" — *The Bellevue Literary Journal*
"Snow in the Chihuahuan Desert" — *Texas Weather Anthology*, Lamar University Press
"Pickers" and "Miracle in Falfurria" — *Huizache*
"The Month of Mary, 1974" — first published with *Mujeres de Maiz Literary Journal*, and published by *Mezcla; Art and Writing from The Tumblewords Project*
"Easter Sunday, 1975" — *BorderSenses*
"Tearing Down" — *The Texas Review* and *Acentos Review*
"In the Name of Progress," and "Inventory — off Horizon Blvd." — *The Texas Review*
"Inventory — off Horizon Blvd." — *Odes & Elegies: Eco-Poetry from the Texas Gulf Coast*, Anthology, Lamar University Press
"On Route 290" — Texas Poetry Assignment

To Margaret Randall, Katherine Hoerth, ire'ne lara silva, for reading and reviewing the two manuscripts that became one: *Cracked Spaces*. To the Friday night writing group: Raquel Mejia, Julia Quintanar, Lucille Hopple, and Almendra Voladora, and the morning writers: Dr. Gina Nuñez, Dr. Diana Riviera, and Diana Becerra. To JD Pluecker, Dr. Juana Moriel, Dr. Johnny Payne, for your support and input. To Miguel Lopez Lemus, artist extraordinaire and editor. To Octavio Quintanilla: Thank you for allowing your artwork to grace the cover of this book. Finally, to my husband and daughter, for your understanding and patience on days I was engrossed in writing. Ian and Anna, for your editorial acuity; to Danny, for accompanying me to my poetry readings.

For my parents, Luis and Manuela

"We transform the *posos*, apertures, *barrancas,*
abismos that we are forced to speak from.
Only then can we make a home out of the cracks."
                                        —*Gloria Anzaldúa*

Contents

I.

A photograph, transfer, and memory. A still life and conversation. A child's record and cricket, in an album and postcard. In the child's box, the chirp and peal. Was it the fog, or scissors? Or the legs rubbing against the mother. Focused on the spatter. Of grease. Of crayons. Of the unseen and seen future. The child's markings in walls. In her eyes' blind spot. On the stoned walls. The child extends his arms. Sums up the cricket. To a point of meet, mouth, teeth, tongue. The cricket's pulse in his hands. All the while, the mother lost in thought.

American Me

for my dad

Crossed the bridge in '55
In faded blues, Fruit of the Loom
Shirt on my back.

For a twenty and a five
Bought a U.S. Visa
Este tirilon, ranchero,

Watermelon-eating Mexicano
From the Valley of Guadalupe.
Spit-shine calcos,

Brillantina slick-back hair,
My spit and comb ready.
Can't catch me unprepared.

For cinco clemos took
The trolley to La Plaza
De Los Lagartos, where

The alligators live
Under Chinese Elms.
Took a taxi

To San Eli to pick pecans,

Build pig pens, stir adobes,

To live on thank yous and maybes.

Then bussed my ass

To Okie town to the onion fields

Of Bakersfield.

Kissed your white land,

Broke my back, sweated tears,

For a piece of the American dream.

February 23rd is anniversary day

I crossed the border.

Not a lick of English

To prove me right.

Still smell the onions

On my fingertips.

Pickers

for Nina, who refused to leave restaurants until served.

Open-mouthed, my little sister gapes at butter
commercials the way I stare at stars —

Stars witnessing who we are, where we'll be
next season, picking cantaloupe and berries.

Plucking the stray stem of a lily wedged in weeds,
waiting for a child to nip it and set it free.

Come spring, we'll be pinching strawberries
in fields thick with fog. My eyes wandering

to children, in the distance, pedaling hard
on their way home from school, unmindful

of our backs bend to the shape of piety, picking
their fruit. But the stars know. And the lilies.

And the birds perched on wires who watch
our fingertips the color of blood.

In summer, we'll be in the Arizona heat, pass
canyons and towns bleached from too much light.

Their welcome signs wilt in the heat. We'll stop
for a meal. But neither our humility nor money

will buy smiles. Places will tell us: We don't serve
Mexicans. Through dark desert coddled under righteous

light, we'll make our way home. And I'll never
see stars the way I did before.

Month of Mary, 1974

We stop for a photo in front of our house
on our way to see the Virgencita
to offer yarrow from Abuela's garden.

In the picture,
we're a blur of white organza.

Our house, in the background,
      rises like a birthmark —
      the only one for miles.

Each May, in the absence
of rain, we splash with the rhythm
of curling water from the hose.

But we are children with dreams —
      we want to tousle like luchadoras
         in deep puddles,
         in rain-gutted roads,
      like children we read
      in school books.

What we know is parched skin,
    cracked heel,
        every cell silent and ashy
        in the tamarindo-heat days.

What we know is a hazed horizon,
    a blue sky unaccountable
    for its guttural purr —
        that promise of rain.

What we know is May when we recycle
    our First Communion dresses.

We walk to church. The path patched with brittle
    grass and gray-green foliage
    of desert marigolds.

Each May, Mary awaits our return. Our flowers.
    Our mouths. When we murmur prayers,

    deep from the breast
        of our thirst.

Easter Sunday, 1975

Decked out—como dicen—

    in our Easter vestidos, patent-

        leather shoes,

        eyelet ruffle socks.

We are muñecas de aparador.

Our skin, caramel smooth, in varied

    shades. Pressed against the fabric,

        our breasts. Like knots. Our eyes

 devoid of expression, except

    for a glint of amusement.

Como Mom wanted us to be—

She blamed the U.S.

for our fracasos. Said life would've been different.

We would've been different. *If* she had stayed

in Mexico.

If thirty years later,

    the divorces—

If the children out of wedlock—

If the mental breakdowns—

If we would've lowered our eyes,

                our lustful gaze—

If we hadn't wanted so much—

If we would've been like coat hangers

                without questions—

If we would've just stayed like muñecas—

Somedays, we wonder, like her, if

Mexico would've saved us.

Why You Are Here

On my cracked tongue, I taste the grove
Of oranges. The spine of trenches covered
In strawberries, moisten by Pacific water.
On its shore, it makes my body shiver.

And I think of you, 80 year old, henchman of
History, under a Chinaberry in mid-July, swatting
Flies, sweat seeping from your furrowed forehead.
I think of you, back home, back curved,

How you plow the field behind my house,
As if you are plotting my future. Clearing,
Plucking the bad pits like in a bible story.
Except you don't purge fruitless saplings.

You nurture them because like you, like me,
Like most of humanity, we need a second chance.
We know a crooked spine left without support
Stays twisted for perpetuity —

Legs and arms wracked. A horse limps.
A hoe's shaft splinters.
That's why you're here, in mid-July,
With the sun on your weary spine.

California Dream

With a trimmed belly, my father leans
on his 59 Chevy, rolled sleeves over
cut biceps. Behind him, the orange
grove. Pitched rooftops of neighbors'
homes. What I see is not the eucalyptus
shouldering his body. What I see is him.
Thirty years later, he'll tell me I would've
loved California —

      the bay's white chest,

        the checkered fields, how the night

        implodes with citrus scent.

His history clings to me like grape skins
to teeth. I shapeshift to solidarity.
From pecan groves to avocado orchards,
I want to see what he sees —
a white-washed bungalow,
my mother skinning nopal paddles,
my grandmother smoking corn husks,
my grandfather rolling buttons, readying
for poker day.

My father's California comes to me
in a dream. She's a long-legged woman
in fishnet stockings.
She's a man — dark-skinned,

> flat-bellied,

> white-teethed —

> seducing me to come.

A Girl Missing Her Mother the First Time She's Away from Home

My mother's panic paces my medulla — the place where she lodges.
Then, insomnia, at dawn. I slip my body into the solitary pool.
Float on my back, weightless, like smoke.

My mother is a comet — a falling star.
I wade the cool water. I think heaven is a solitary country.
Loneliness licks my throat, and at 3:06 A.M., I dial home.

My mother is the night air — hot on my skin.
I'm hypnotized by the bluish stratosphere of water.
Water reminds me of her — the moist of her kiss on my cheek,
A jar of water in her hands to quench my thirst.

My mother is Jupiter. Moon. Venus. Mars. A planet waiting
To be discovered. I butterfly across the pool. Sky's turning
Pink. I sink my body down. Enter the warmth. Close my eyes.
And I'm inside my mother's womb.

El Patriarca

I hear your tongue click at the end of a line as a key clinks and clanks in the mouth of a keyhole. Click. As a cricket's thighs rub against each other for want of love. In the kitchen, I listen to my sisters' chatter, how they've lost their chime. You say I don't love you enough to listen to an old man's stories of conquests. How under the guise of darkness, you waited to plow and slice the earth, open, then rip exoskeletons of sleeping beetles, offering them to a greedy sun. I see your tongue's tip slip between your teeth, the color of buff. This is not a daughter's love for a father — her country. You see, I've picked off the bur of your lies. I'm no longer the ear that wants to hear your tongue: Click, Click, Click its way back to my heart. I am not a beetle you can excise or command to wake as if it's a new dawn.

II.

This morning, a nature walk. Before the raptor frights the rabbits into submission. The sun scurries the rattle to return to rocks. Three blister beetles circle one dead fly. How it died? the child asks. One dead fly. All it wanted was to fly. In the distance, a roadrunner. Frozen. But for its nervous eye. Behind the brush, the child still asks, then cries. How to explain why.

State of Affairs

1

When the snake sleeps,
A woman slips silently into a river.
She is a stranger in the palm of a desert.
And the sun, with an unnameable face, calls
The roll. Claims her hour.
A hawks circle above.

2

Between thumb of dust and rain,
The clatter of hundreds swirls above
The marketplace. All humanity is visible.
A bomb detonates. A woman screams.
A man deconstructs
The art of details.

3

A halo rises from grass rooftops.
Boys hidden in ashes leave
Their village, survive on mud —
Urine mixed with sand.

In the fissure of borders,

They leave fragments of bones.

It's not uncommon for boys

To bury their brothers.

Looking at Her Father

I watch you raise the spoon
To your mouth on evenings we sit
For dinner when the nickel dust is washed
Off your skin, the work shirt is exchanged
For a t-shirt. I note the expanse of chest,
Your biceps bulge under frayed material.
I want to be swung above your head,
To feel your strength.

When I'm older, I'll visit the metal shop
Where you work — steel fighting between
Your arms, against your chest — . Din of
Machines agonizes inside my ears. Dust
Of metals decadent in the bludgeoning heat.
I see your chiseled body, your clenched jaw,
Your hardened fists on days you couldn't stand
Our noise. Years later, I'll seek a softer man.

One Day in San Antonio

Left El Paso in a rush to meet you
Under the cottonwood trees. Eight hours later,
I'm here, in the San Antonio heat,
Clothes clinging to my body. Eyeing the Alamo
Across the street from my hotel room, I say
These gringos deleted our story from the history
Books. You kiss me. Say we have a story
To make. You press your hips to mine. I remind you
I'm a Mexican; you're a gringo. And there's the question
Of stolen lands. Of where you stand. It's more than just
About a damn fort. Christ, how I want to make you into
Every white man, every hand who raised a whip
To my people's back. To make you pay
For the wrongs done to this land. For now, I'll turn
The other cheek, divert my eyes away from
The glaring lies. Shut off the voices that whisper:
Malinchista   *Malinchista*   *Malinchista*

Canto: The City I Love

I

I was asked what business I had in Juárez by a man who parked my
car at the All Day Parking $3, under the vault of Puente Lerdo.

I crossed the bridge in heels, listened to distant hymns of amor to
Dios from a cathedral. Red-potted geraniums in clay pots, dotted
Avenida Juárez. Pimped up the concrete-slab walls, the peeling
paint of shops. Piñatas and sombreros slung from doorways to
entice sales.

The city is almost quiescent. Almost slipping into the bluewing of
sleep.

At dawn, federales skimmed off the rot from streets only brave
souls sauntered after dark.

This is how I remember you. Country of my ancestors. Pinched
cerros in the distance, long stretch of snaking roads. The scent of
coming home. Before the stirrings of death.

If I call it pain. Don't touch it — the wound left on the sidewalk
where her body fell, gunned down by sicarios.

Tattooed on her back, in the center of a red heart, her message: *Amo. Amor. Te amo.*

Her death, like clemencia and castigo. Her death— a child of Tlazoltéolt.

The night of her death was the color of an unrecoverable violet.

It's a good thing you died, Abuela, before the stirrings of death....

II

I opened my eyes to shadows on my window cast by the Chinaberry tree. Grandfather hated Chinaberries. Said they attracted lechuzas—witches who cast love spells on men and inflict pain on their wives.

When visiting, he'd asked my mother to burn down our tree.

We visited his mother's grave on Día de Los Muertos. I'd sit next to her. Extracted the weeds from her home.

Graves: the arteries to our past. Umbilical walls of our memory. Before the stirrings of death. Before clavicles, breasts, pelvises littered the outskirts.

My grandfather and I walked the bricked-paved plaza. Fed silver-blue pigeons gutted papaya and sweet bread while we drank Aguas Frescas. This is how I remember you —

Before the city drowned its sorrows in the melancholy sighs of old men.

Before whispers of mothers fell upon us, and the Río Grande channeled their rage to memory. Their message: *Escribe todo. No dejes que olviden la muertes de nuestras hijas.*

III
Madre,
I dream of you;
Dream of the night of your skin.
Your Indian hands folded into patience.
What I want is a fist. Or hands
opened to a jaw. Clamped down.
Its teeth to monsters who scavenge
In shadows, refusing regret.

Madonna,
Buoyant in a river
Of transgressions, the pillage still rises,
Many years later, still rises.

Still, bones are scattered.

Still, I love this country.

Still, I love,

      love,

           love.

IV

Women march knee-deep in justice. Raised in air, fists bruise space;

they bruise the walls and doors; the songs they sing are wounds.

My breath, hovers, drifts into a pained cloud, hoping someone will

catch it — this siren of mothers.

The Boy Who Played with Fire

Those sunglasses seal your face with secrecy. I sense your gaze
Upon me. You measure my fear — such silliness. I've known you
All my life. How you hammered street corners onto your soles.

Named each pothole. Every alley, your territory, your escape
From home. Love was not in chords of your songs — those
Corridos mules sang on the way to the drop-off.

Now, you walk a relentless rhythm. Like wind before rain one
Obeys. Despite the rumors. The body count that rises. You know
The question is the wait. How will you know when the world's

Foot goes under. Will you be one drop of much water? Another
Wasted life. For now, you are fearsome. A boy teasing greed
And mortality. Everything in passing punished by your presence.

Día de muertas

1

The exact location where she rests
      Is in the fissured boundary
Of two nations.

In a barbwire corrido
      Of wall. In an ofrenda.
           In a halo of tears.
             In daily rituals.
               In the godless.
In the spirit of a tree. In the night air
      That loosens hair ribbons.
             In a spider's web. In the moon's shoulders.
           In the shape of a cloud.
               In shallows of the Río Grande.

2

She was lucky if her bones
Were found. *If* she were lucky,

She'd be inside a casket
Of pressed pine. Or,
She would've shapeshifted to

A butterfly,
Flown across the Río's water

Where she now lives, happily,
After the American dream —

If she'd been paying attention,
She would've read the billboards —

                              ¡Ojo!

And cinched her own safety.

3

The Río carries the weight
Of Death. Not water.
The weight of unearthly
Light. A script. An envelope.
A phone number pinned
Inside.

The Río carries the shadow
Of a shapeless cloud. Tiny
Houses of families afloat.
A hologram
Of names that weigh it
Down.

The Río carries sangre. Sorrow.

Silence. Sirens. With the dead,

Yields to the stretched belly

Of the gulf to come to

Rest.

4

My friend asks: Has the Río ever carried life?

5

It could've been your daughter

Or mine

In the street corner, where she waited

For a green light

To cross the street for home.

It could've been your daughter

Or mine

Working the nightshift

Being followed

The night she disappeared.

It could've been your daughter

Or mine

Writing poetry as an act

Of defense. Defiance.

The day she was gunned down.

It could've been your daughter

Or mine

Or mine

Or mine

Or ours.

Message

1

Eyes closed stretched limbs stiff
On a bed you died a sweet death
At the wake of sky thick with black
Smoke, severed breasts, and semi-
Automatics discharged by broken
Children and santa muerte strung-
Up devotees who butcher
And sacrifice for the promise
Of dollars: big house, big truck,
Big stamp of drug lords carved
On bones to scare the hell out
Of old ladies with a message:
Keep your prayers, flags, Virgin,
Rallies — this won't do
The women, children, nation
On the way to dust.

2

Abuela, my love, it's good you died
And everything you knew
Has grown into darkness
That remains unpunished.

The sun doesn't touch deeper

Than the skyline. I pray the way

I know how:

> *Dear Lord, send down a spiral of whoop ass*
>
> *Upon those who defecate your country.*
>
> *Amen.*

3

In the streets:

Tears of mothers

Piss of dogs

Bullet holes of drug lords

Ache of grandmothers

Remains of daughters

Grieved mother country

Who guards your streets

Of cocaine and decay?

Beautiful

Behind the desk the doctor is sure
Of himself when he utters I will not
Get better because no one does with
These things not when the mind has given
Up the way mine does some days
Even when everything is beautiful.

And I ask him to define *beautiful*
Because the word is abstract
And the word, that word
Is not enough for me to grasp what
He means when he says I will never be
What I was —

Red Lipstick

I wear red lipstick, blood-red matte.

My 5-year-old niece says lipstick

Is for old ladies; that's what her mother

Says — her mother of 22, with lips gleaming

Raspberry gloss. Then, my niece

Puts on her Beats. Next time

I go to the drugstore; I look for gloss

On sale, pick a soft-spoken pink,

For that's what I am — soft, since

I've been spoken for, for twenty years.

And even before my cassette tape

Bellowed a Flock of Seagulls's song,

And The Cure crooned Just Like Heaven,

My red-lipsticked mouth curled for want

Of a smoke, and a boy who trashed, head-

Banged on stage. Like my best-friend's boy

She met at the club when she said she'd found

Her man — stoned, rum and coke in one hand.

By 2 A.M., she was sitting on his lap, his hands

Between her thighs. Lips on her neck. Her hair

Matted to her scalp. She'd looked at him

Like someone studying a passport. Sometimes

I remind myself of those days — a mirage,

When we wandered thirsty, lost, hungry —
For love. Those days when red lipstick
Was the rage.

Snow in the Chihuahuan Desert

A fit of snow like a tantrum despite the sun's persistence

in December, when trees unveil remnants of summer's

escapades and love stories. The desert is clothed in winter's

white for hours, grasses wear its armor, and life retreats

to burrows. Beneath creosotes, the clamor of birds

cease, and we are high like winds in spring. Crazy

with want to touch, to lick, devour the sky's uncoiling,

as if we were young again when mother, on her knees,

kneaded snow like flour, rolled the half-inch layer to

a snowman. Its limbs like my body, weak and boney,

punctuated with blood each month. Every cycle a tearful

story. My body prayed to die. Now the girl is dead. My

mother is frail, still kneads flour to dough for the warm

tortillas she bakes for breakfast. December comes, each year

heavy for want of snow. But it's only desire. For nothing, not

nostalgia, not prayer resurrects those days of white.

Yellow Light

I've left the birds' songs outside. Let them spread their spiel
Over the collar of neighbors mowing their turfs.
Besides me
Is the steady panting of the mutt,
The percolating old coffee maker willing itself
      To fill one last time its 10-cup drip
      As if its life depended on it—
                  It does.

In the kitchen, the onomatopoeia of
A fly. I watch
The American flag like a flayed skin, oscillating in the wind.

There's memory in wind—
Some winds more unsettling than others.

Spring out West—
Hot days and dust—wind hissed like a snake
Outside the windows. The incoming light
—singular, blinding, bouncing, swallowing
The last of the moisture off my skin.
The walls— inside/out—saturated
With a one-sentence, long paragraph

Of light. I stopped to reflect the imperfections

Of the wall I painted cranberry — the wall,

A plaster mix of cement and half-moon strokes.

When C.D. Wright died, I cried. Pushed a small

Bookshelf against the cranberry wall,

And shelved her books there — only hers.

I meditated on the day we traveled across

The South. At night, against the shadows

Of cypress and macrame of Spanish moss,

Swaying in a mild breeze, like ghosts along

A two-lane highway.

The bone healer is watching, I said to my children, their eye

Sockets visible in the dark — fear and awe at once.

I chanted:

> *Deepstep Come Shining*
>> *Deepstep Come Shining*
>>> *Deepstep Come Shining**

Their tiny bodies curled

Against the back

Of the seat. They had had enough

Of the South,

Its Beloveds who inhabit the woods.

"The atmosphere observes its own light," Didion writes.

Inside where I reside to write,
I turn the recess
Lights on before
Darkness sucks in the morning's
Glow.
 The trees' shadows escape
The incoming thunderstorm. Didion's book by my side
— Marksman of words —
 Amplifies the fatalism
 Of this dark, as if
 I will take to fever and die as if
 I am not aware of how Southern light yellows.
 Like when the Trinity River turns murky when it rains.
 How everything around me seeds
 From its waters.

*Title of the book by C.D. Wright.

III.

Twist of dry air on singed leaves. Cranberry sun. No chance of rain. Last summer the last almond tree died. Crazed and curled under three digits and rising. Death is a cap. A trap in the desert. A promise. Desert people check the sky for a smudge, a bruise, a synonym for maybe. Gnaw on the stripped bone of distant thunder. Like inchworms, suspended. From dry blades. We toss our heads here and there, exhausting our days. In panic.

Blessed

for the ancestors

We pass colonias— homes cast together
Like unplanned meals, anchored
To hard soil. Dogs in front yards,
Skinny as threads, eyes forlorn,
Tethered to a distant line of horizon.

We pass this land of littered yucca pods
Like fists, with skin leathered and calloused.
Raptors glide above this desolation
That might as well be our souls.

We pull to the shoulder to watch
A jackrabbit jump into a creosote's embrace
To escape the winged shadow of
The migra bird constantly
Weaving,
Returning,
Circling,
Diving,
Lower and lower,
Down to tufts of dreams, where panic peels

Layers of joy — yet another theme
As to why you came here —

Like a Teresa of Avila's prayer
You brought with you:
Your hands,
Your eyes,
Your feet,
Your body,
The litany of you.

For the others with no feet,
no eyes, no hands, no body
no heart
Like yours to work this earth
as you do.

Inside the coolness
Of our car, we ponder
Our luck
To have made it out
From under the gaze
Of this singular light.

Away
From parched arroyos,

Comatose rattlesnakes,

Sunburnt backs,

Pillows of dust,

Dirt roads,

Caliche breezes,

Where nothing ever happens

But to panicked roadrunners

And burrowing lone bees

Who share the ghost of what was—

A Rachel Carson's sea

Her pen would caress

With poetry.

Then, Beloved, hear our prayer:

Blessed are we who never crossed

The Río Grande in a moonless night.

Blessed are we who were never smuggled

Under blankets in a truck's bed.

Blessed are we whose bodies were left

Unscathed by an orchard's owner.

Blessed are we who are dreamers.

Our breasts,

Our song,

Our sun,

Our language

Affixed to our soul like a snug belt.

All because you gave

Your body for us.

Unfinished Texas Poem

to marshland to origami vines

to piney woods to undulating dunes

to limestone caves

to monochromatic corridors of desert

to arroyos tethered to mountainsides, to backbones

of huichaze

to canyons and craters

to bays, bogs, rivers

to rocky hills, dancing devils in the pandhandle

to plains and forgotten trails

to Franklin

to Guadalupe

to Fort Davis

to Chinati

to Caddo, Carrizo, and Coahuilteco

to Kiowa, Kitsai, and Karankawa

to Wichita, Bidai, and Jumano

to Apache and Tiguas

to Tawakoni and Tonkawa

to incandescent city lights

to paint, concrete, quaint and charm

and mammoth shopping complexes

to El Paso

to San Antonio

to Houston and Galveston

to Austin

to Corpus Christi

to Brownsville

to Dallas/ Fort Worth

to Lubbock

to McAllen

to the Gulf of Mexico...

Tearing Down

When the dozers break the spine
of yuccas, bury the creosote, the sap

of soaps under plans for another
subdivision, where do the burrow owls go,

the lavish tarantulas, the sweeping paws
of roadrunners and slender mice?

When the raptor disappears amid rising clouds
of sand, and cataracts sweep the last of

dung beetles, no mounds of brush to hold
the rain cheerfully back. When all is dust

and concrete, what will be left to astonish?

About That Light

While out West
In its keynote light,
In a desert stripped
Of its flora,
Almost every inch of land
Is now a tiny house
With a tiny yard—

While in the South,
In its narrow band of light,
I clean my eyeglasses twice.
Every inch
A forest, bog, stream.
Houses warped
In lost footing of earth,
Left to decompose
In algae-filled air—

Inventory — off Horizon Blvd.

rose-colored couch slipping
off side of sand dune, broken
beer bottles parrot a puzzle in
progress, two yards away pink
barbie car missing front wheel,
absent dowel pins, Styrofoam
cup hooked to yucca's needle,
red-tailed hawk over area, 3x4
5-inch deep, jagged-edged concrete
slab, "fuck you" in black, sharpie
pen, core spilling on snakeweed,
ticking in wind. other trash:
                a bottomless chair.

In the Name of Progress

1

What is left are dunes
arranged by wind, an occasional hawk's
cry, cleaving gossamer
sky. Famished
for holy flesh.

When the animals left their names —
            Couch's Spadefoot, Crevice Spiny, Aztec's Rail —
years disappeared, knowledge left,
into a weathered unknown.

2

My brother fills a bucket with water
every night, sets it on the other side
of the rock wall that surrounds
his property. He waits for the roadrunners,
coyote and its babes. At night, he listens
to thirsty tongues lapping up water
their bodies ache to fill.

3

We wouldn't stop the cord

of roads, then houses, then knots

of legs and feet moving farther, roaming

everywhere, nothing sleeping

in the parched desert.

4

What kind of game is this? Insatiable

greed sweeping land in the name

of progress, coaxing infinity into

our backyards. Always wanting something

else even as the green and blue bleed out.

Miracle in Falfurrias

And the ladies pray to St. Isadore

        For rain

    Lauds in the morning

        Lauds in the evening

      A congregation of eyes fastened to the cross

To the saint of stone and paint and rain

    And the farmer irrigates

His bone-dry land

    Three stones away from death,

       His crops

Then it rains, downpour

    From the fingertips of clouds

      From laden cataracts

        Of the Beholder

Rainstorm: cascade: cloudburst: monsoon

Floods the corn, the cotton

Decays

     In the newspaper's headlines:

"DELUGE: Farmers Pray for Rain to End"

On Route 290

A type of Juniper. Nothing clear and cut. Bikman Organic Farm
then Bell Farms. What's ahead? Bogs D'Arc Lane. Corn and more
shucks of corn, and in between, no shaft for light. In the hurricane
sky. A semi-truck t-boned my sister sixty miles away.

We're in Klaus Lane now, across seventy-seven acres. We slaughter
down this country lane, zoned for BP, KFC, DQ, HEB, and whatever
else builds this way. Stop at the Breakfast Basket for biscuits and
gravy. She got banged up—an imprint of round cheek and broad
nose on the driver's windowpane.

Ahead is Dog Trail, but we must cross Watermelon Fest and Old
Potato Road. Here is a trickle of goats. Longhorns and more horns.
There's Friendship Cemetery, with stones and water holes. Said she
was on her way to pick a buddy from the airport, flying from
Tombstone.

A row of windmills. The orange glow of corn. Soon to be
subdivided.

In Gilding, close to Whistle Stop next to Magnolia where the trees
are wider. This must be God's country. A sign reads: All trucks
enter here. In his defense, the driver who hit her had a history of

depression. But he was caked with amphetamines and on parole that day.

We stop at Carmine. Rows of antique shops line the sidewalks. At Round Top, in the center of Main Street, a white cow lingers, then moos its way to Memory Lane. Before she passed out, she called Mom. Said she was afraid; could she fly home?

We take a shortcut to Crossover. Hempstead skirts Heartbreak. Turtle Bayou is drowned in Trinity water while the young, humped trees in Winnie clamor under catcalls of cicadas. She remembers nothing while in the hospital, except her bruised knees; she's happy she made it out.

In the South, a hanging

Of anything is reminiscent of other hangings.

Texas, in Jasper in '98, a black man dragged,
Chained to a pick-up truck. I gazed at the TV screen —
A sightseer, an onlooker compounded by
The ambivalent distance, the lapse of time,
A song in the background.

Then the murder of 24 paisanos — mi gente,
      In El Paso, 2019 — not lynched, not hung, but gunned down
            For the color of their skin.

      Like catching a whiff from the malodorous sewers,
      Like a rope around the throat, I understood then,
      This violence not bound to static, but sipping
      Drop by drop into cracks of the space I called home.
      And I wanted to be there to touch its broken rocks.
      I wanted to take the form of someone with no soul —

Your death will leave a trail.
Your life will disappear like sound that rises in air —

            Poof! Then gone.

Our anger, black smoke, stencils the sky. We ask:

Why?

Pink

for the sisters, cousins, lovers, best friends, and daughters we've lost

Pink is the color of crosses

Pink is the color of disappeared daughters

Pink is the color of femicides

Pink is the color of mothers

Pink is the color of my cousin

Pink is the color of my cousin's daughter left without her mother

Pink is the color of lament

Pink is the color of injustice

Pink is the color of murder

Pink is the color of pain

Pink is the color of the spot where their bodies dropped

Pink is the color of mourning

Pink is the color of victims

Pink is the color of the oppressed

Pink is the color of the marginalized

Pink is the color of the young maquila woman whose body was

dumped in the desert

Pink is the color of brutality

Pink is the color of domestic violence

Pink is the color of rape

Pink is the color of dismembered bodies

Pink is the color of the women who were gunned down for standing up to injustice

Pink is the color smoke

Pink is the color of their names

Cracked Spaces

1

When I seek to empty the weight of my new life, I go home.
Shed. Transform into trinity. Bathe in the pools of
my mother's eyes. Lie down with the life I used to know.
My belly hungry for family. All the rooms familiar.
Their doors tugging patiently at my hands to open.

2

When the day's heat reaches me, I'm its vessel. Streaks of
uncertainty are only momentary. The heat is inside me.
And I'm my mother's daughter; my father's daughter;
my ancestors' daughter. I'm this country's daughter.
And the border — this pause between us — is a place
to catch my breath.

3

Here's the Río Grande I've swum. Here's the sun I'm intimate
with — its familiar gaze upon my skin. Here's the whir of sand
at the door, begging to enter. Here are my hands, palms opened,
reaching to touch your crinkled, cracked earth. The face of your sky.

4

Now the sky begins its blush. From Rim Road, I see El Paso opening

its pretty mouth. Flashing teeth of flickering lights. Bandwidths

of desert breeze carry the evening. Some sing

this city is a city of no hope—lamentable chords. When I sing

to differ. How this city embraces our migratory souls. Our wounds

and abrasions. Our death and light. In her swollen belly's warmth.

In her open mouth. In her fissures, I build a life.

M. Miranda Maloney's Biography

M. Miranda Maloney is a writer, publisher, and editor. She is the founder of Mouthfeel Press, one of the first bilingual presses in the U.S.-Mexico border to publish emerging and established poets from the U.S. and South America, writing in Spanish and English. She is also the Outreach Educational Coordinator for the Smithsonian Latino Center Digital Collections and poetry editor for *BorderSenses*, and editor at Arte Público Press. Her poetry, essays, and articles have appeared in the *Bellevue Literary Journal, Huizache, The Texas Review, Mujeres de Maiz, The Más Tequila Review, Acentos Review, Tasteful Rude*, and anthologized in various publications by Lamar University Press, among others. Her work has been translated into Spanish and published in Uruguay, Mexico, and Italy. She has edited over 20 collections of poetry and short stories. Her book, *Lost Letters of Mileva* (Pandora Lobo Press, Chicago, IL), was translated to Spanish and published by Yauguru editorial in Uruguay in 2019. *Cracked Spaces* (Pandora Lobo Estepario Press) is her most recent collection. She grew up in Socorro, Texas, a small town on the outskirts of El Paso, Texas. She currently lives in East Texas. Miranda Maloney received her MFA in Bilingual Creative Writing from the University of Texas at El Paso and has been a literary activist for over 20 years. She is currently working on her third collection *The Moon in Her Eyes*.

About *Cracked Spaces*

In *Cracked Spaces*, by M. Miranda Maloney, the reader is faced with the search for identity. The collection of poems reflects upon the social classes, racial issues, changes in linguistic codes, gender issues, religious perspectives to crossing the border, among other questions that invite us to examine our own position in society. Belonging or not belonging, reinventing oneself in new universes permeates each poem. The family is present, the origins, the perspectives of the mother, the daughter, the grandmothers, the memory, and questions of the patriarchal paradigms. The poetic voice tries to find its place to understand who it is and where it fits. From the personal it moves to the public, and we read poems about the dead of Juárez. The poetic space created in *Cracked Spaces* invites the reader to constantly inquire about her own place in the world. This is a searching reading that confronts, heals, and that I would read over and over again.

En Cracked Spaces, de M. Miranda Maloney, el lector se enfrenta a la búsqueda de la identidad. La colección de poemas reflexiona sobre las clases sociales, cuestiones raciales, cambios en los códigos lingüísticos, cuestiones de género, perspectivas religiosas al cruzar la frontera, entre otras cuestiones que nos invitan a examinar nuestra propia posición en la sociedad. Pertenecer o no pertenecer, reinventarse en nuevos universos impregna cada poema. La familia está presente, los orígenes, las perspectivas de la madre, la hija, las abuelas, la memoria y las cuestiones de los paradigmas patriarcales. La voz poética intenta encontrar su lugar para entender quién es y dónde encaja. Desde lo personal se traslada al público, y leemos poemas sobre los muertos de Juárez. El espacio poético creado en Cracked Spaces invita al lector a indagar constantemente sobre su propio lugar en el mundo. Esta es una lectura inquisitiva que confronta, sana y que yo leería una y otra vez

—*Xánath Caraza*, author of *Exercise in the Darkness / An Exercise in the Darkness*

Title: Cracked Spaces
Author: M. Miranda Maloney
Cover image: Octavio Quintanilla
Cover design: Sandra Salas.
Editor: Miguel López Lemus (Editorial Pandora Lobo
Estepario Productions)

About the cover image

Title: Tejidos del mismo hilo
Author: Octavio Quintanilla.
Size: 11x14
Medium: Archival ink on acid free paper

Pandora Lobo Estepario Productions Publications

- **Cantología I** (Anthology)
- **Noche de Colibríes** by Xanath Caraza,
- **The Rhythm of Every Day Things** by Sandra Santiago,
- **The Lost Letters of Mileva** by M. Miranda Maloney,
- **Poems and Photographs 2004** by Kalina Fleming Lopez,
- **Unveiling the Mind by Beatriz** Badikian-Gartler,
- **Chiaroscuro** by Álvaro Torres-Calderón,
- **Body Maps** by Elga Rategui Zumaeta,
- **Corazón Pintado** by Xanath Caraza (2015)
- **ENTROPÍA versus ARMONÍA** "Memoria del Éter"/ ENTROPHY versus HARMONY "Memory of the Ether" by Ivonne Sánchez Barea. (2015)
- **Aunque la nieve caiga de repente** by Jorge García de la Fe (2015)
- **Cielo de Magnolias, cielo de silencios** by Olivia Maciel Edelman (2015)
- **Tinta negra/Black Ink** by Xánath Caraza, translated by Sandra Kingery. (2016)
- **Dreaming Rhythms, Despertando silencios** by Carmen Bardeguez-Brown (2016)
- **Mantras para bailar** de Álvaro Hernando. (2016)
- **Corazon de hojalata/Tin Heart** by Margarita Saona (2017)
- **Mar en los huesos** de Juana Iris Goergen (2017)
- **El cuaderno del pendolista** de Federico Palomera Güez (2017)
- **De los peces la Sed** de Silvia Goldman (2018)
- **Chicago Express** de Álvaro Hernando. (2018)
- **Balamku** de Xanath Caraza (2019)
- **Tinta Negra Μαύρη μελάνη** de Xanath Caraza (2019)
- **Relatos Diplomáticos** de Dixon Acosta Medellín (2019)
- **Tiempo Eterno/Timeless** de Rosalba Henao (2020)
- **Ejercicio en la oscuridad/An exercise in the darkness** de Xanath Caraza (2021)
- **Cracked Spaces** by M. Miranda Maloney (2021)

EDITORIAL
Pandora Lobo Estepario Productions™
http://www.loboestepario.com/press
Chicago/Oaxaca
2021

www.ingramcontent.com/pod-product-compliance
Lightning Source LLC
Chambersburg PA
CBHW051515260626
47162CB00008B/2980